FASCINATING SCIENCE PROJECTS

EVERYDAY CHEMICALS

Sally Hewitt

Franklin Watts
London • Sydney

© Aladdin Books Ltd 2003
Produced by
Aladdin Books Ltd
28 Percy Street
London W1T 2BZ

ISBN 0–7496–4955–0

First published in Great Britain in 2003 by
Franklin Watts
96 Leonard Street
London
EC2A 4XD

Designers:
Flick, Book Design and Graphics
Pete Bennett

Editor:
Harriet Brown

Illustrators:
Ian Thompson,
Catherine Ward and Peter Wilks – SGA
Cartoons: Tony Kenyon – BL Kearley

Consultant:
Dr Bryson Gore

Printed in UAE

A CIP catalogue record for this book is available
from the British Library.

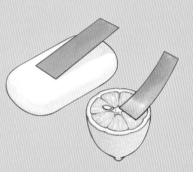

Contents

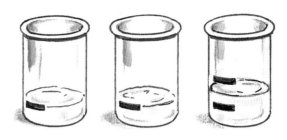

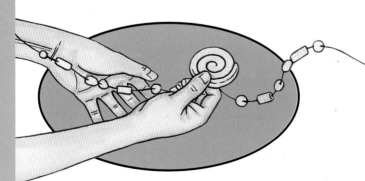

Introduction

In this book, the science of chemistry is explained through a series of fascinating projects and experiments. Each chapter deals with a different topic on chemistry, such as making gas or oxidation, and contains a major project that is fully supported by simple experiments, 'Magic' panels and 'Fascinating fact' boxes. At the end of every chapter is an explanation of what has happened and the science behind it. Projects requiring the use of sharp tools, heat or chemicals should be done with adult supervision.

This states the purpose of the project

METHOD NOTES
Helpful hints on things to remember when carrying out your project.

Materials

In this box is a full list of the items needed to carry out each of the main projects.

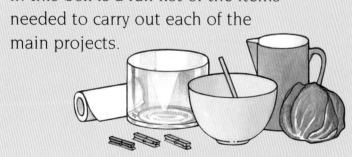

Figure 1

1. The steps that describe how to carry out each project are listed clearly as numbered points.

2. Where there are illustrations to help you understand the instructions, the text refers to them as Figure 1, etc.

Figure 2

THE AMAZING MAGIC PANEL
This heading states what is happening

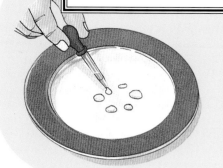

These boxes contain an activity or experiment that has a particularly dramatic or surprising result!

WHY IT WORKS
You can find out exactly what happened here.

WHAT THIS SHOWS

These boxes, which are headed either 'What this shows' or 'Why it works', contain an explanation of what should happen during your project, why it happened and the meaning of the result.

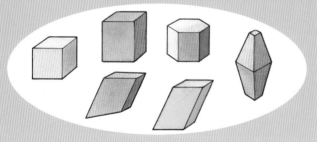

Fascinating facts!
An amusing or surprising fact related to the theme of the chapter.

Where the project involves using a sharp knife or anything else that requires adult supervision, you will see this warning symbol.

The text in these circles links the theme of the topic in each chapter from one page to the next.

What is a chemical?

Chemicals are made of atoms. Simple chemical substances are made up of just one kind of atom and are called elements. When two or more atoms are held together a molecule is formed. Elements or molecules can be combined to make a large number of different chemicals. Chemists study chemicals and use them in reactions. Chemists often produce other chemicals in these reactions. Chemicals can be changed by adding heat or pressure, or by mixing them together.

Be a chemist and make slime

METHOD NOTES
Experiment with the amount of Borax to get the right consistency of the slime.

Materials
- warm water
- a measuring jug
- a plastic jug
- PVA (white glue)
- a wooden spoon and a teaspoon
- food colouring
- Borax (available from a pharmacy)

1. Measure out 30 ml of warm water in a measuring jug. Pour it into the plastic jug (Figure 1).

2. Measure out 30 ml of PVA glue (white glue) and add it to the warm water in the jug (Figure 1).

Figure 1

6

Figure 2

3. Mix the glue and water together using the wooden spoon (Figure 2). The glue should be evenly spread throughout the water. Add a few drops of food colouring.

4. Now measure out 100 ml of warm water. Add 2 teaspoons of Borax to it (Figure 3) and stir until the Borax disappears.

5. Add 1 teaspoon of the Borax and water to the glue and water (Figure 4). Mix everything together vigorously.

Figure 3   **Figure 4**

6. You can make the slime thicker by adding more Borax and water.

7. Knead the slime as if it were bread dough. Now the slime is ready for you to have fun with (Figure 5).

WHAT THIS SHOWS

The molecules that make up glue, Borax and water have been mixed together. The change that took place was a physical change. This physical reaction created your new substance – slime. PVA glue is a kind of plastic. The molecules that make up plastic are held together in long chains called polymers. When you add the Borax it tangles up these chains, and water gets trapped in the tangles. The result is a thick, jelly-like substance that feels very strange. Push and pull the slime and watch how it moves. Make sure you store your slime in a clean covered container to keep it moist.

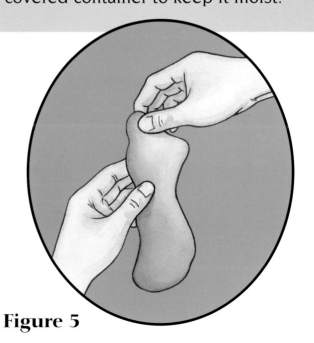

Figure 5

7

To make slime, the chemicals you mixed together changed physically. Other substances are made up of a mixture of chemicals that don't change when they are mixed.

What is a chemical?

MIX AND UN-MIX A MIXTURE

Make a mixture of sand, uncooked rice and water (Figure 1). Stir it all together in a bowl. Carefully pour the mixture through a sieve into a jar (Figure 2). The sand and water pour through the holes. The rice is left in the sieve, so you have separated the rice from the mixture.

Now fold a coffee filter paper into a funnel and place the funnel in a jar (Figure 3). Pour the sand and water mixture into the funnel (Figure 4). The water goes through the filter paper and the sand is left behind.

Figure 1

Figure 2

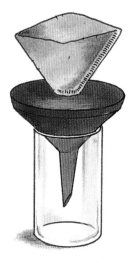

Figure 3

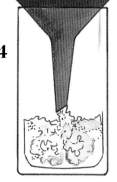

Figure 4

WHAT THIS SHOWS

Even though you have mixed sand, water and rice together, it is possible to separate them. You un-mix the mixture by passing it through different size holes. The chemicals themselves do not change.

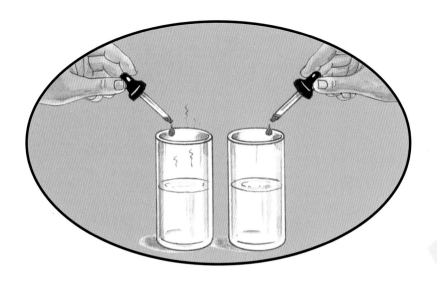

MOLECULES ON THE MOVE

Add a few drops of food colouring to a glass of cold water and a glass of hot water. Watch the colour sink through the water. After a while, the drop of colour spreads all through the water. This happens because water molecules are always on the move. They bump into the tiny particles of colour and spread them around. Molecules of hot water move faster than molecules of cold water, and make the colour spread more quickly.

Making gold
The first chemists were called alchemists. Their experiments were based on science and magic. They thought they could find fame and fortune by turning ordinary metal into gold. Sadly, this is impossible!

Absolutely everything is made of atoms. Some chemicals change their physical structure when they are mixed together and some don't. It is possible to un-mix some mixtures.

Solid, liquid & gas

The particles of any substance are made from one or more atoms held together. How the particles are held together determines whether it is a solid, a liquid or a gas. The atoms in solids are held together very strongly, so solids keep their shape and cannot be easily squashed into a smaller space. The atoms in liquids are held together less strongly. Liquids flow and change shape, but cannot be squashed easily. Gas particles are held together weakly, so gases flow and can be squashed.

Make ice cream to see a liquid turn into a solid

METHOD NOTES
To speed up the process, put your mixture in the freezer before packing it in ice and salt.

Materials
- a coffee can
- 250 ml milk
- 250 ml cream
- 125 g sugar
- flavouring and a spoon
- a larger bowl or can
- a towel
- crushed ice and salt

1. Put the milk, cream, sugar and any flavouring you choose in a clean can (Figure 1). Stir it together slowly and steadily.

Figure 1

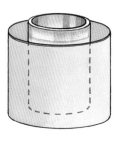

Figure 2

2. Place the can full of ice cream mixture inside the larger bowl or can (Figure 2).

Figure 3

Figure 4

3. Wrap a towel around the outside of the bowl (Figure 3).

4. Pack the crushed ice around the can and sprinkle salt on the ice (Figure 4). Don't get any salt in the ice cream.

5. Start stirring the mixture (Figure 5) – it takes about 30 minutes, so get a friend to help. The mixture will thicken into tasty ice cream (Figure 6).

WHAT THIS SHOWS

Freezing a liquid turns it into a solid block. A solid block of ice cream would not be easy to eat. If you didn't stir your ice cream, this is what would happen. As your ice cream gets colder, particles of ice start to form. Stirring the ice cream as it freezes breaks the ice up into small pieces. The bits of ice get smaller and the ice cream gets smoother the more you stir. Stirring also causes air to become trapped in the mixture and helps to make the ice cream light. The secret of good ice cream is to keep stirring. Try making different ice cream flavours, or try adding chunks of chocolate or sweets.

Figure 5

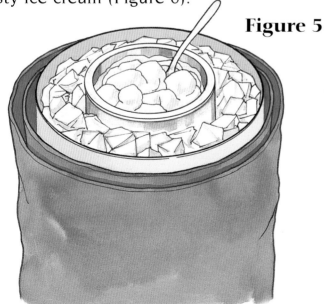

Figure 6

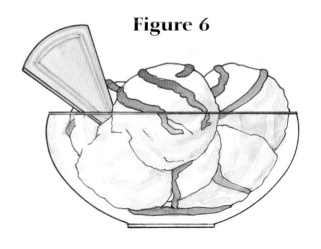

11

Solid, liquid & gas

Water can exist in three different phases. It changes from one phase to another – solid, to liquid, to gas, or vice versa – when heat is added or taken away.

THE PHASE CHANGES OF WATER

Add some food colouring to water in an ice cube tray and freeze it. Seal one ice cube in a clear plastic food bag (Figure 1). Put the bag on a cake rack over a bowl of hot water (Figure 2). The ice cube will melt.

Figure 1

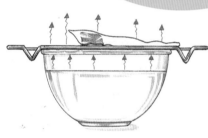

Figure 2

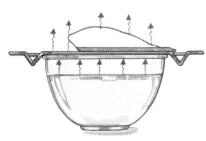

Figure 3

A small amount of the water turns into a gas called water vapour, and the air in the bag heats up. Watch the bag expand (Figure 3). Take the bag off the rack and the vapour becomes water again (Figure 4).

Figure 4

WHAT THIS SHOWS

Very cold water molecules move slowly and join together to form ice. When they are heated, the molecules move faster and the ice melts. With more heat, the air and water molecules in the bag move faster still. Some of the water becomes gas.

Solid ponds

In winter, lakes in the far north and south freeze solid. Tiny ice crystals grow bigger and bigger, and join up until the whole surface of the lake is solid ice. Smaller ponds can freeze completely solid!

THE AMAZING GROWING WATER
See water grow as it freezes

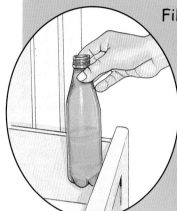

Fill a plastic bottle nearly to the top with water. Put the bottle in the freezer. The next morning, you will see that the water has turned into ice and is pushing out of the top of the bottle.

WHY IT WORKS
Water gets bigger, or expands, when it freezes. This is because there are more empty spaces in ice than in liquid water. So the ice starts to burst out of the bottle.

Figure 1

CHOCOLATE BISCUITS
When chocolate is heated, it melts and becomes liquid. When it cools, it becomes solid again. Break some chocolate into pieces (Figure 1) and put them in a heat-proof bowl. Put the bowl into a saucepan one third filled with water.

Put the saucepan on a low heat and stir the chocolate until it melts (Figure 2). Pour melted chocolate onto some biscuits (Figure 3). Leave them to cool and the chocolate will become solid.

Figure 2

Figure 3

Although water goes through phase changes, it is always water. The chemical make-up of water does not change whether it is a solid, a liquid or a gas.

13

Solutions

When some substances – salt, sugar or bicarbonate of soda, for example – are mixed with water, they dissolve and make a mixture called a solution. When salt dissolves in water, it seems to disappear, but in fact it is still there. You can taste it even though you can't see it. In the water, the salt breaks down into tiny atoms that are too small to see. When water from a salt solution evaporates and turns into a gas in the air, the salt crystals are left behind.

Make crystals from a solution

METHOD NOTES
This experiment works best if you make the solution slowly and patiently.

Materials
- bicarbonate of soda
- hot water
- a glass jar
- pipe cleaner
- a teaspoon
- a pencil

1. Stir the bicarbonate of soda into half a jar of hot water, 1 teaspoon at a time (Figure 1). This makes your solution.
2. Stir the solution until the soda disappears before you add the next teaspoon.

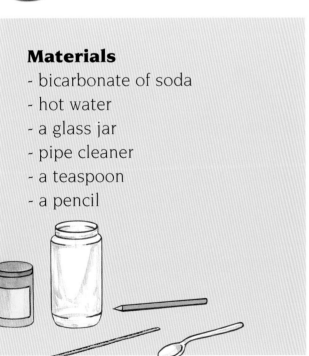

Figure 1

14

Figure 2

3. Keep adding the soda until it stops disappearing. This means the solution is saturated and can dissolve no more soda.

4. Bend one end of a pipe cleaner into an interesting shape (Figure 2). Curl the other end around a pencil. Balance the pencil on the jar and suspend the pipe cleaner in the solution (Figure 3).

5. The next morning you should see sparkling crystals on the pipe cleaner.

Figure 3

WHY THIS WORKS

Hot water can hold more soda molecules than cold water. As the water cools down, molecules of soda leave the solution. The only place they have to go is to attach themselves to each other and the pipe cleaner.

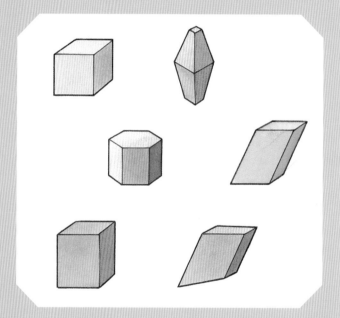

The crystals grow as other soda molecules are attracted to them. They cluster together on the pipe cleaner to form large, sparkling crystals. Do this experiment again making solutions using water with salt, sugar and washing soda. Examine the many different shaped crystals through a magnifying glass.

Solutions

Molecules come in all kinds of different shapes and sizes. Some molecules fit very closely together. Others are larger and more unevenly shaped, with spaces between them.

MAKE A MOLECULE MODEL

This model will help you to understand what happens when you make a solution. Pack a glass jar with marbles (Figure 1). It seems to be full. Now pour in as much sand as you can (Figure 2).

Figure 1

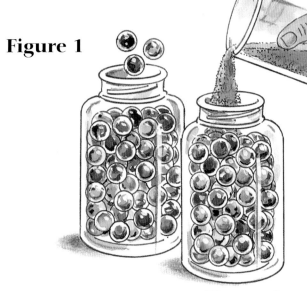

Figure 2

You will be surprised how much sand fits into the spaces between the marbles. Water molecules are like the marbles. They are not packed tightly together and there are spaces between them. Salt molecules are like the sand. They fit into the spaces between the water molecules.

People sit on water!
The Dead Sea, in Israel, is one of the saltiest lakes in the world. There is such a high concentration of salt in this solution that people can float in it without even having to swim.

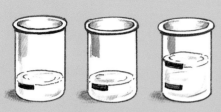

Take two clear film canisters and put one tablespoon of water into each. Pour both canisters into one. Mark the level of the liquid. Repeat the experiment using the same canisters, one tablespoon of water and one of rubbing alcohol (see page 20).

The liquid doesn't reach the mark!
WHY IT WORKS
There is less liquid than you started with, because the water molecules fit into the spaces between the rubbing alcohol molecules.

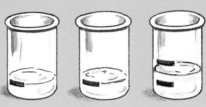

Figure 1

SEPARATE A SOLUTION

Mix salt, a teaspoon at a time, into a jar of hot water, until it dissolves (Figure 1). This makes a salt solution. Pour the solution into a shallow saucer (Figure 2). Put the saucer in a warm sunny spot and leave it for a day. The water will disappear, leaving salt crystals behind on the saucer.

Figure 2

WHY IT WORKS
When the water warms up in the Sun, it evaporates – turns into water vapour. It rises into the air and leaves the salt behind on the saucer.

When a substance dissolves in a liquid, it makes a solution. Sea water is a solution of salt and water. Salt can be separated from the water by evaporation.

Mixing liquids

Water, oil and honey are all liquids. They need a container to hold them. They take on the shape of the container they are in. Liquids flow in different ways. Water splashes when you pour it, but honey moves slowly. Viscosity is used to describe how thick a liquid is. A thick liquid that flows slowly is said to be viscous. Liquids also have different densities – honey is denser than water. This means that a certain amount of honey, 250 ml for example, is heavier than 250 ml of water.

Experimenting with layers of liquid

METHOD NOTES
Pour the liquids slowly so they run down the side of the container.

Materials
- 3 plastic cups
- runny honey
- vegetable oil
- water
- kitchen scales
- a tall clear container
- food colouring

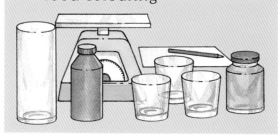

1. Half fill 3 plastic cups – one with honey, one with vegetable oil and one with water (Figure 1). Make sure you have the same amount of liquid in each cup. You can put a few drops of food colouring in the water to make it easier to see.

Figure 1

18

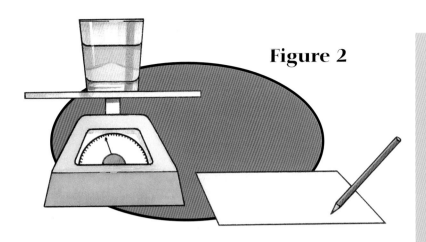

Figure 2

2. Weigh each cup and write down the weights (Figure 2).

3. Pour the heaviest liquid – the honey – into the tall container and let it settle.

4. Then carefully pour in the next heaviest liquid – the water – so it lies on top of the honey.

5. Slowly pour the lightest liquid – the oil – on top of the water to make the final layer (Figure 3).

Figure 3

Why not try making layers with milk, salty water and washing up liquid and see whether the results are the same.

WHAT THIS SHOWS

In this experiment, the liquids lie on top of each other in layers and don't mix together. The quantity of liquid in each cup is the same, yet honey is the heaviest. This means that honey is denser than water and oil. So it forms the bottom layer. The cup of water is lighter than honey but heavier than oil. So it forms the middle layer. Oil is the least dense of all three liquids and forms the top layer. Usually, the denser a liquid, the closer together the molecules are packed.

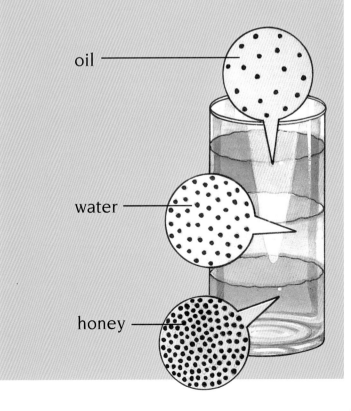

oil

water

honey

Figure 2

Figure 3

Mixing liquids

MAKE AN OIL BUBBLE

You can use rubbing alcohol for this experiment. Rubbing alcohol is often available from chemists but if you can't find it, most nail varnish removers work as well. Half fill a small jar with coloured water. Carefully float a blob of oil on top of the water (Figure 1).

Figure 1

Slowly trickle some rubbing alcohol down the side of the jar until the blob of oil forms two or three bubbles (Figure 2). Watch the bubbles of oil settle in the middle of the coloured water (Figure 3). Put the lid on the jar. Without shaking it, put the jar in the light on a windowsill.

WHAT THIS SHOWS

When you add the rubbing alcohol to the water, you make a solution. As you add the rubbing alcohol, the density of the solution changes. Once it has reached the same density as the oil, the oil hovers in the middle. The solution pushes against the oil from all sides so it becomes round.

TERRIFIED OIL
See detergent repel oil

Use a dropper to place drops of oil in a circle around the middle of a bowl of water. Wash the dropper and use it to place a drop of detergent in the middle of the circle. Watch the blobs of oil rush away from the detergent to the edge of the bowl.

WHY IT WORKS
The blob of detergent breaks the surface tension – the skin of the water – in the centre of the bowl. Unbroken water tension pulls the blobs of oil out to the edge of the bowl. They look as though they are terrified of the detergent!

Detergent! An amazing new discovery
Until about 50 years ago, people couldn't buy detergent – chemically-synthesised soap. Imagine how difficult it was to get rid of all the dirt and grease using regular soap!

Liquids have different densities and viscosities. Some liquids mix and make solutions. Others, like oil and water, don't mix at all.

Acids & alkalis

There are three main groups of chemicals – acids, alkalis and neutrals. It is often useful to know whether the chemicals we use every day in the bathroom and in the kitchen are acidic or alkaline, and how strong they are. Acids are usually sour to taste and alkalis are usually bitter. Because some are very strong it is not safe to taste or touch them! Instead, we can use a colour-changing chemical reaction to discover what is in a substance.

Make indicator brew and test substances

METHOD NOTES
You can tear the cabbage leaves instead of using a knife.

Materials
- a red cabbage
- a knife
- a chopping board
- boiling water
- 2 bowls
- kitchen towel
- a wooden spoon
- pegs
- string
- milk and soap
- lemon juice
- bicarbonate of soda

1. Ask an adult to help you chop the cabbage. Put it in one of the bowls (Figure 1).
2. Carefully pour boiling (very hot) water onto it (Figure 2). Stir it slowly using the wooden spoon. The colour from the cabbage dissolves in the hot water and turns it blue.

Figure 1

Figure 2

3. Pour the water into another bowl (Figure 3).

4. Let the blue water cool. You have made an indicator liquid that will tell you whether a substance is acid, alkali or neutral.

5. Cut the kitchen towel into strips and dip the strips in the indicator liquid (Figure 4).

6. Use the pegs to hang the strips on the string until they are dry (Figure 5).

7. Dip the indicator strips into soap, milk, lemon juice, and bicarbonate of soda mixed with water. Different substances turn the paper different colours (Figure 6).

Figure 3

Figure 4

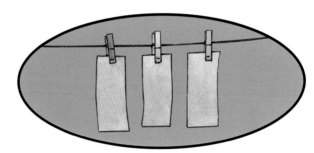

Figure 5

WHAT THIS SHOWS

Substances that are acidic, like lemon juice, turn the blue indicator strips pink. Those that are alkaline, like bicarbonate of soda, turn the strips green. Other substances, like soap, water and milk, are neither acidic nor alkaline. They are neutral and don't change the colour of the indicator paper.

Figure 6

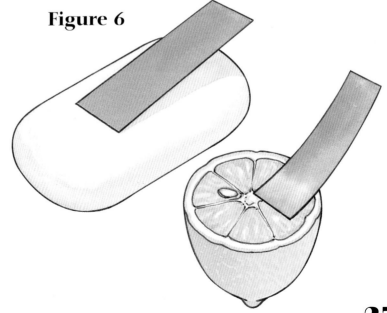

23

Acids & alkalis

Indicator paper is also used to test perfumes, lotions and make-up to make sure they will not harm our skin. Other kinds of indicator paper are made with plants or even with fungi.

MAGIC PAINTING

Dip some sheets of absorbent white paper in the indicator liquid you made on page 22. Spread them out on a cake rack to dry (Figure 1). Mix some water and bicarbonate of soda in a glass (Figure 2).

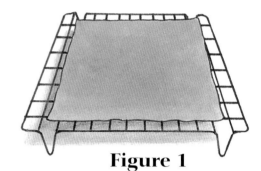

Figure 1

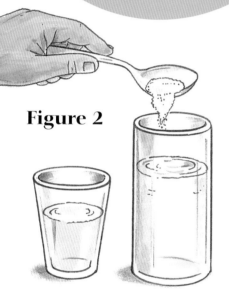

Figure 2

Pour some vinegar in another glass. When the blue paper has completely dried you can paint on it (Figure 3). The bicarbonate of soda and vinegar make magic paints that turn the paper green and pink. Try painting over the green with vinegar and the pink with the bicarbonate of soda solution.

WHAT THIS SHOWS

The vinegar is an acid and turns the indicator pink. The bicarbonate of soda solution is alkaline and turns the paper green. Some acids and alkalis are stronger than others and turn the indicator different shades of pink and green.

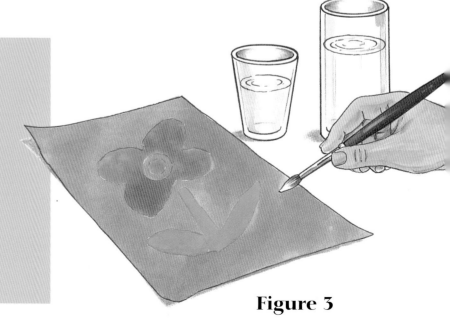

Figure 3

THE AMAZING MYSTERY BREW
See your indicator brew magically change colour

Half fill a glass with blue indicator liquid. Pour in some vinegar. As if by magic, the liquid turns red. Now sprinkle in a teaspoon of bicarbonate of soda. The liquid turns blue again!

WHY IT WORKS
Vinegar is an acid so it turns the indicator liquid pink. Bicarbonate of soda is alkaline. When you add an alkali to an acid, it neutralises the liquid. That's why the bicarbonate of soda turns the liquid blue again.

Figure 1

PINK LEMONADE

Pour some of the indicator liquid you made on page 22 into an ice cube tray (Figure 1). Put the ice cube tray into the freezer overnight. Once the liquid has frozen, take out two ice cubes and add them to a glass of lemonade (Figure 2). They will turn the lemonade into a strange pink drink. This happens because lemonade is acid and the indicator ice cubes turn it pink.

Figure 2

Why don't you make indicator liquids from red onions, peach skins or beetroot. You will find that all kinds of plants contain colour-changing chemicals.

Some acids and alkalis are strong and harmful. An indicator tells us if a substance is acid or alkaline. Some indicators can tell us how strong an acid or alkali is to help us use chemicals safely.

Chemical reactions

Different things can happen when chemicals are mixed together. Sometimes they make a mixture. Air is an example of a mixture of gases whose molecules don't react together or change. Sometimes chemicals make a solution. Sea water is an example of a solution of water and salt. Sometimes when chemicals mix there is a chemical reaction. When this happens the molecules of the chemicals are rearranged and a chemical change takes place.

Make a chemical change

METHOD NOTES
Never pour plaster of Paris down the drain. It will harden and block the pipes.

Materials
- plaster of Paris
- a large container or bowl
- water
- a wooden spoon
- an old rubber glove
- clothes pegs and string
- washing-up liquid

1. Pour a cup of plaster of Paris into the bowl. Gradually add half a cup of water, stirring all the time (Figure 1). Make sure there are no lumps.
2. Keep stirring until the mixture is smooth. It is then ready to pour into the mould.

Figure 1

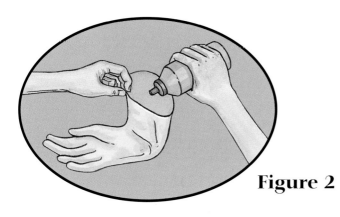

Figure 2

3. Put a few drops of washing-up liquid into the rubber glove (Figure 2). Rub the glove between your hands so the liquid coats the inside.

4. Pour the plaster of Paris into the glove (Figure 3). Press it into the fingertips.

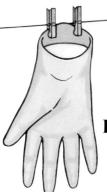

Figure 3

Figure 4

WHAT THIS SHOWS

When plaster of Paris and water mix, a type of chemical reaction takes place. The molecules rearrange and make a new substance. The glove feels warm because heat energy is released while this change is happening. Plaster of Paris is great for model making. It stays liquid just long enough after you add water to mould it into an interesting shape. Once it has set as hard as rock, you can't easily change its shape again.

Figure 5

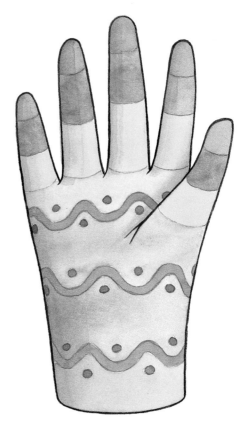

5. Hang the glove on a line with clothes pegs (Figure 4) and leave it for about 30 minutes. The glove will feel warm while it is setting.

6. When the plaster of Paris has dried hard, peel off the glove and remove a model of a hand (Figure 5). Why not paint your model?

Chemical reactions

COAT A NAIL WITH COPPER

Pour 120 ml of white distilled vinegar into a glass jar and add a pinch of salt (Figure 1). Drop about twenty well-used copper pennies covered in tarnish into the jar (Figure 2). Now scrub an iron nail with scouring powder until it is really clean and shiny (Figure 3). Rinse it thoroughly with cold water.

Figure 1

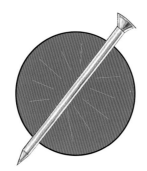

Figure 2   **Figure 3**

Drop the nail into the jar with the pennies (Figure 4) and leave it overnight. In the morning you will find that the pennies are shining and clean. The nail will be covered in a coat of a gold-coloured metal called copper (Figure 5). Be careful when you get rid of the liquid – it is poisonous.

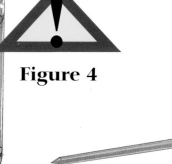

Figure 4

WHAT THIS SHOWS

The vinegar and salt dissolve the tarnish on the copper pennies. This process releases tiny particles with electric charges called ions into the vinegar. The copper ions react with the iron in the nail and cover it with copper.

Figure 5

THE AMAZING EGG
See vinegar dissolve an eggshell

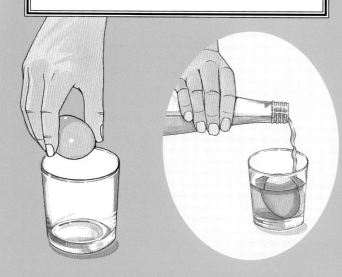

Put an uncooked egg in its shell in a glass and completely cover it with vinegar. After three days, very carefully take out the egg and hold it up to the light – you have a see-through egg! The dark blob in the middle is the yolk.

WHY IT WORKS

The vinegar reacts with the shell and dissolves it. It doesn't dissolve the thin skin called the membrane that holds the egg white and the yolk in shape. You have used a chemical reaction to remove the eggshell without breaking the egg.

Children's toy invented by mistake! During the second world war, it was difficult to get rubber. While experimenting with chemicals to create a substitute, a scientist accidentally created a new substance...Silly Putty!

Chemical reactions change substances. Plaster of Paris hardens, eggshells dissolve in vinegar, metals are coated with copper, and new substances are discovered – all because of chemical reactions.

Making gas

There are all kinds of different gases. The air around us is a mixture of a number of different gases including nitrogen, oxygen and carbon dioxide. Oxygen in the air is essential for life. The gases in air are invisible and have no smell. Some gases are harmful. Exhaust fumes, for example, are poisonous gases made when cars burn petrol. Like exhaust fumes, many different gases are produced by chemical reactions.

Mix chemicals to make magic foaming brew

METHOD NOTES
Make sure the cauldron-shaped pot is on a tray before you add the vinegar.

Materials
- water and bicarbonate of soda
- washing up liquid
- a cauldron shaped pot
- vinegar, a jug and a large bowl
- sequins and glitter
- food colouring
- kitchen scales

1. Weigh 50 g of bicarbonate of soda and put it in a large bowl.
2. Sprinkle sparkling glitter and shiny sequins onto the bicarbonate of soda to make your brew look magical (Figure 1).

Figure 1

30

Figure 2

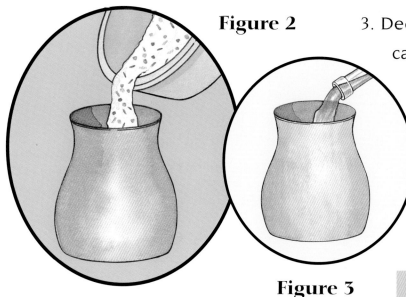

3. Decorate the pot to look like a witch's cauldron. Pour the sparkly mixture into the cauldron (Figure 2).

4. Mix 125 ml of water, 60 ml washing-up liquid and a few drops of food colouring all together in the jug.

5. Add this sparkly mixture to the cauldron.

Figure 3

6. Now make sure the cauldron is on a tray or draining board – you are about to make a mess!

7. Pour the vinegar into the cauldron (Figure 3). Watch the magical brew bubble up and pour over the sides of the cauldron (Figure 4). Listen to it fizz!

Figure 4

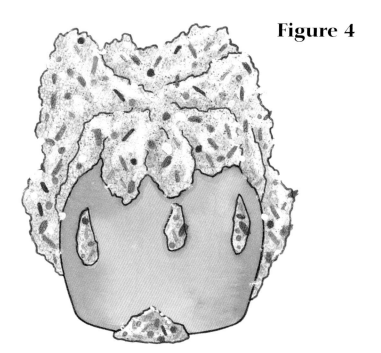

WHAT THIS SHOWS

The two magic ingredients are the bicarbonate of soda and the vinegar. Vinegar is acidic and bicarbonate of soda is alkaline. When they mix, a chemical reaction takes place and they make a new substance – carbon dioxide gas.

The carbon dioxide gas and the washing-up liquid create thousands of bubbles which fill the mixture and push it out of the cauldron. The fizzing that you hear is the sound of bubbles bursting as they try to get out of the cauldron.

Making gas

Gases are put to many uses. Gas is added to drinks to make them fizzy. Some gases are burned as fuels, but others can be used to put out fires.

PUT OUT FIRE WITH CARBON DIOXIDE

Push six used matches into either side of a piece of cork and fix a birthday cake candle on top (Figure 1). Pour enough water into a jar for the cork to float on. Carefully light the candle with a long taper (Figure 2).

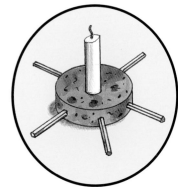

Figure 1

Figure 2

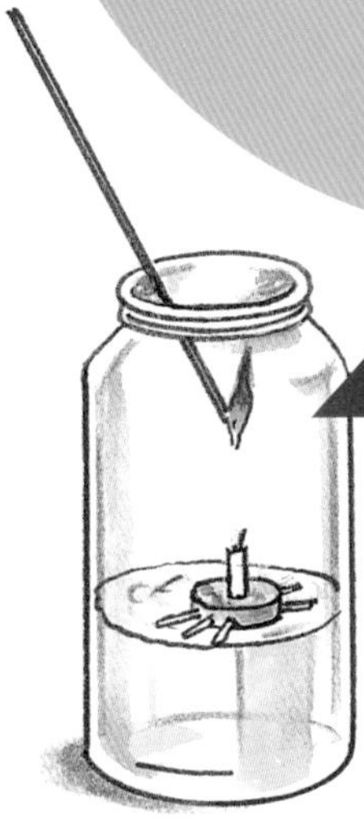

Add about 50 g of bicarbonate of soda to the water and stir it (Figure 3). Quickly add about 125 ml of vinegar to the jar, being careful not to put out the flame (Figure 4). The mixture will fizz and, after a few moments, the candle will go out (Figure 5).

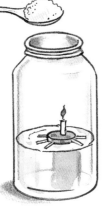

Figure 3

Figure 4

Figure 5

WHY IT WORKS

The vinegar and bicarbonate of soda react to make carbon dioxide bubbles, which rise and push air out of the jar. A flame cannot burn without oxygen in the air, so the candle goes out.

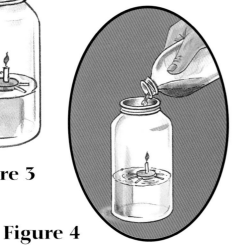

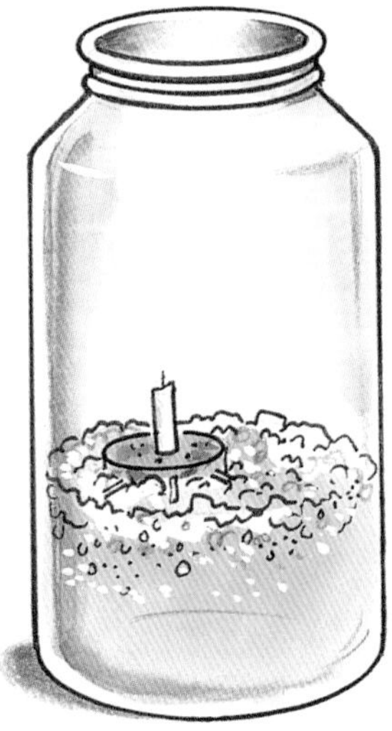

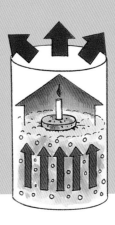

Figure 1

Figure 2

MAKE RAISINS DANCE

Open a new bottle or can of fizzy drink. Pour some into a glass jar. Tip some raisins into the jar (Figure 1). Watch them dance up and down. If you look closely you will be able to see bubbles clinging to the raisins (Figure 2). Can you see that the ones going up have more bubbles on them than the ones that are sinking?

WHY IT WORKS

Bubbles cling to surfaces. The bubbles of carbon dioxide in the drink cling to the raisins and carry them up to the top of the jar. The bubbles pop and the raisins fall. More bubbles stick to them, carry them up again and keep them dancing.

Gas can make you sleep!
Nitrous oxide is a gas that is used as an anaesthetic – it can be used to put a person to sleep before minor surgery. It is also called laughing gas as it makes some people laugh!

Some gases are made by chemical reactions and by heating chemicals. Some gases have no smell and others are smelly. Gases can be poisonous and even explosive.

Heat

Heat can cause a chemical to change physically. Adding heat causes solids to melt and liquids to turn into gas. Taking heat away causes liquids to become solid or freeze into solid blocks. Chemical changes are also brought about by heat. We bake soft bread, cake and pastry mixtures in the oven to make them firm or crispy. Flour and water dough becomes hard when it is baked. Heat is also produced by some chemical reactions, such as when plaster of Paris sets hard (see page 27).

Bake dough to make jewellery

METHOD NOTES
Keep your hands sprinkled with flour to stop the dough from sticking to them.

Materials
- 200 g of flour
- a large bowl
- a jug of water
- a wooden spoon
- a kebab skewer
- thread
- a baking tray
- paint

1. Put the flour into the bowl. Use the spoon to make a well in the middle. Gradually pour water into the well, stirring it into the flour as you go until you get a soft dough (Figure 1).

2. Knead the dough with your hands to push out trapped air (Figure 2).

Figure 1

Figure 2

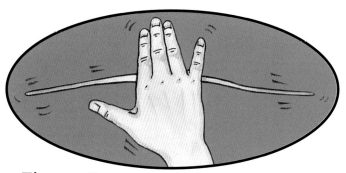

Figure 3

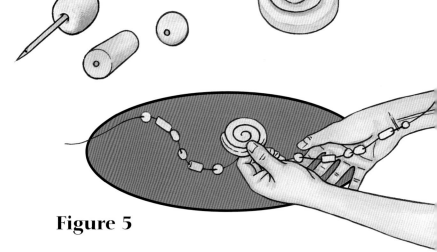

Figure 4

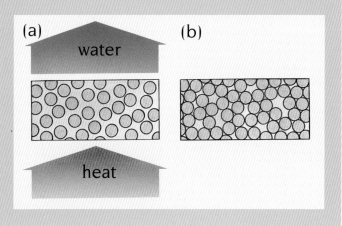

Figure 5

3. Sprinkle flour onto the work top. Mould the dough to make beads.

4. Roll out a sausage shape (Figure 3) and curl it round to make a pendant.

5. Push the kebab skewer through each bead to make a hole (Figure 4).

6. Put the beads on a baking tray and bake them slowly in a warm oven so they harden right through.

7. Let the beads cool then thread them to make a necklace (Figure 5). Paint the beads to make your necklace colourful (Figure 6).

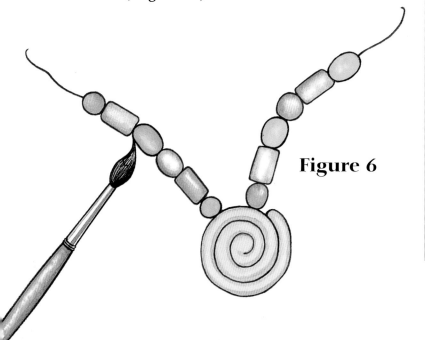

Figure 6

WHAT THIS SHOWS

In your dough, the flour molecules are suspended in the water. When dough is still, it keeps its shape like a solid. It moves like a liquid when you push it. (a) When you bake dough, heat makes the water molecules evaporate. (b) When the water is gone, the dough is hard and solid. Your beads are tough and will keep their shape.

(a)

water

(b)

heat

Heat

We add or take away heat when we prepare food. We take heat away from milk, cream and sugar to make ice cream. We add heat to milk and flour to thicken sauces.

MAKE CUSTARD

Put 1 tablespoon of custard powder and half a tablespoon of sugar into a bowl. Gradually add 250 ml of milk, stirring all the time to make the mixture smooth (Figure 1).

Figure 1

Put the mixture into a saucepan and stir it over a low heat, until it thickens into smooth custard (Figure 2). Pour it onto fruit to make a delicious pudding.

Figure 2

WHAT THIS SHOWS

Custard powder is corn flour – a kind of starch. Heat causes the starch molecules to unravel. The starch molecules then tangle and trap the liquid, making the custard thick. The more custard powder you use, the thicker the custard will be.

Fireworks are burning chemicals

A firework is packed with powdered chemicals. Light the blue touchpaper and the powder burns, sending out bangs, sparks and colourful flashes. When the chemicals have all burned up, the firework goes out.

THE AMAZING INVISIBLE WRITING
Use heat to make writing appear

Squeeze some lemon juice into a glass. Dip a clean paintbrush into the lemon juice and write a secret message on plain white paper. Hold the paper in front of a warm radiator for a few minutes. The writing magically appears!

WHY IT WORKS
Lemon juice burns at quite a low temperature. It turns brown in the heat, revealing the message, long before the paper would burn.

MAKE TOAST

To make toast, heat a slice of bread evenly on both sides. A toaster does this for you and pops the toast up when it is done. Perfect toast is golden brown on the outside and still soft in the middle. Burnt toast is black and hard (Figure 1). But why does it go black?

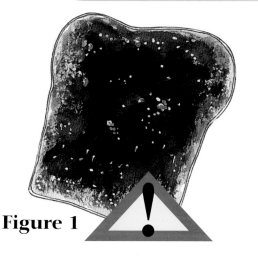

Figure 1

WHAT THIS SHOWS
Molecules of bread contain carbon. When you burn toast, these molecules break down and leave pure carbon on the surface of the bread. When this happens, smelly smoke made up of pure carbon fills the kitchen.

Heating chemicals can cause them to change. We use heat to make changes every day in the kitchen when we cook. When enough heat is added to a substance, it will burn.

Kitchen chemistry

A kitchen is like a chemistry laboratory. The ingredients in the kitchen cupboard are the chemicals. You learnt that custard contains starches that cause it to thicken and turn partly solid, that vinegar and lemon juice are acids and that bicarbonate of soda is an alkali. The fridge, cooker, and food processor are like scientific instruments that take away or add heat, or chop and mix ingredients. Here are more experiments to help you learn about the chemicals in your cupboard.

Make crazy custard – very strange stuff

METHOD NOTES
Don't use instant custard, which has sugar and dried milk added to it.

Materials
- custard powder or corn flour
- kitchen scales
- a bowl
- a measuring jug
- water
- a spoon

1. Measure out 175 g of custard powder. Put the custard powder in the bowl (Figure 1).

2. Measure 125 ml of water using the measuring jug.

3. Slowly add the water (Figure 2). Stir it to make a strange yellow dough.

Figure 1

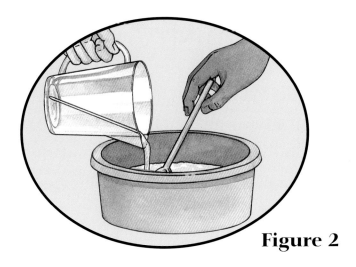

Figure 2

4. Add more water or custard powder until you get the right consistency.

5. Touch the crazy custard gently and feel it move about like liquid (Figure 3). Punch it hard and feel how solid it is.

6. Roll the crazy custard into a ball in your hands. Lift one hand away and watch the ball flatten into a pancake.

7. Break off a chunk. It doesn't stretch – it makes a clean break (Figure 4).

WHAT THIS SHOWS

Custard powder is solid. Water is liquid. When you mix them together, you make a suspension. The custard powder grains hang in the water and are spread out evenly. When you move the mixture slowly, the grains stay evenly spaced.

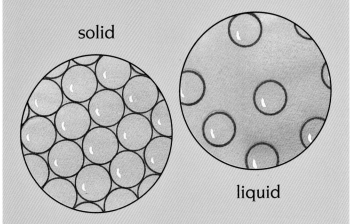

solid

liquid

The crazy custard moves like a liquid. When you touch it quickly, the grains bump into each other and it then behaves like a solid.

Figure 3

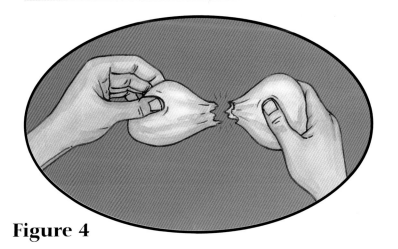

Figure 4

Kitchen chemistry

A colloid is created when bits of one substance float in another. Fog is water droplets floating in air. Whipped cream is air floating in cream. Jelly is water droplets floating in gelatine.

MAKE GELATINE WORMS

Pour a sachet of gelatine into a pan. Ask an adult to help you pour on 150 ml of hot juice. Stir until the gelatine is dissolved. Let it cool. Sink in wide drinking straws so they fill with the mixture (Figure 1). Put the pan in the fridge to set. Roll the fruity wriggling worms (Figure 2) out of the straws with a rolling pin.

Figure 1

Figure 2

WHY IT WORKS

The worms wriggle because they are made of a colloid called a gel. The hot juice breaks up the pattern of gelatine molecules. When the mixture cools, the pattern reforms with a difference – it has liquid trapped within it and a gel is formed.

THE AMAZING MAGIC YEAST
Blow up a balloon with carbon dioxide

Mix together 2 teaspoons of yeast, 1 teaspoon of sugar and 2 tablespoons of warm water in a bottle. Pull a balloon over the bottle opening. Stand it in a bowl of warm water. The balloon magically inflates!

WHY IT WORKS
Heat and water activate microbes in the yeast. As they feed on the sugar, they breathe out carbon dioxide which blows up the balloon.

STIFF STARCH SHAPES

Figure 1

Starch is used to stiffen clothes. Soak lengths of string in a mixture of corn flour, water and food colouring (Figure 1). Remove the strings. Coil them into interesting shapes on a plate. Leave the plate in a warm place. The water will evaporate and leave the starch behind. The starch stiffens the strings so they keep their shape (Figures 2 and 3).

Yuk!
The very first margarine recipe was: "mix warmed beef fat, juices from a pig's stomach, milk and water". However, today margarine is made mostly from vegetable fats and is believed to be healthier than butter.

Figure 2

Figure 3

Try gluing the shapes onto coloured tissue paper. Cut around the shapes and use them to make jewellery or a decoration.

By mixing chemicals from your kitchen, you can create a colloid that acts like a solid and a liquid. You can make a gel and you can activate microbes to make carbon dioxide gas.

Oxidation

As we have learnt, oxygen is one of the gases in the air we breathe. Without oxygen, a fire cannot burn and animals could not survive. Oxygen is also the gas that causes a bicycle to rust by starting a chemical reaction called oxidation. Iron will only rust if oxygen and water are present, so you can save your bike from rust by keeping it dry. Oxidation is also responsible for turning sliced apple brown and for making newspaper turn brown as it gets old.

Discover what makes iron rust

METHOD NOTES
Wire wool is made of iron so it is good for this experiment.

Materials
- 5 glass jars
- wire wool
- salt
- labels
- water
- kitchen towel

1. Put a piece of wire wool into each of the five glass jars. Label the first jar '(a) wire wool + air' (Figure 1).
2. Put the wire wool on some damp kitchen towel in the second jar. Label it '(b) wire wool + air + water' (Figure 2).
3. Add tap water and a pinch of salt to the third jar. Label it '(c) wire wool + air + water + salt' (Figure 3).

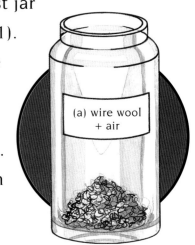

(a) wire wool + air

Figure 1

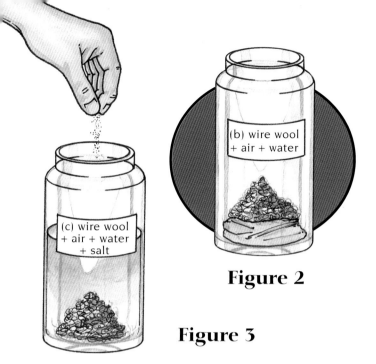

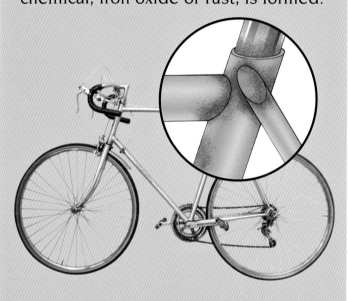

Figure 2

Figure 3

4. Fill the fourth jar to the brim with boiled water. Screw the lid on tightly. Label it '(d) wire wool + water' (Figure 4).

5. Half fill the fifth jar with tap water and label it '(e) wire wool + air + water' (Figure 5). Look at the jars after a week.

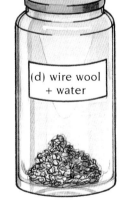

Figure 4

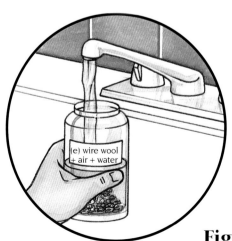

Figure 5

WHAT THIS SHOWS

After a week, the wire wool begins to rust in jar (b) and jar (e), but it rusts the quickest in jar (c). There is little or no sign of rust in jars (a) and (d). When iron in the wire wool is exposed to water and air, a chemical reaction called oxidation takes place and a new chemical, iron oxide or rust, is formed.

Iron needs water and oxygen to rust. Salt in the water causes the iron to rust much more quickly. The wire wool in jar (a) doesn't rust because there is no water in the jar. The wire wool in jar (d) doesn't rust because there is no oxygen in boiled water.

Oxidation

Burning is a chemical reaction that needs three things – heat, fuel and oxygen. Without any one of these ingredients, a fire will not be able to burn.

MAKE AN OIL LAMP

Take a tea light (a night light) out of its metal container (Figure 1). Take out the wick by pulling down on the metal disc it is attached to (Figure 2). Put the wick back in the empty tea light container and carefully half fill it with vegetable oil (Figure 3).

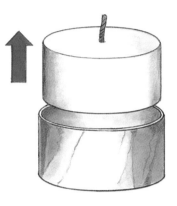

Figure 1

Figure 2

Figure 3

Now ask an adult to help you light the wick using a taper and watch your little oil lamp burn (Figure 4). You have removed the candle wax, which was the tea light's fuel and replaced it with another fuel – vegetable oil.

Figure 4

WHY IT WORKS

The wick soaks up the oil. The heat from the flame on the taper turns the oil into a gas. The combination of fuel, oxygen and heat creates the right conditions to allow the oil lamp to burn.

The never-ending job
Painting the Forth Rail Bridge in Scotland to stop it from rusting, is a job that is never done. As soon as the painting is finished at one end, it has to start again at the other.

BROWN APPLES

Take two quarters of an apple (Figure 1). Coat one of the quarters with lemon juice (Figure 2). Leave both the quarters lying around. You will notice that the one without the lemon juice starts to turn brown while the other remains white.

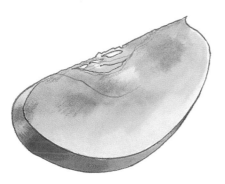

Figure 1

Figure 2

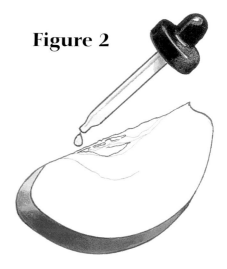

WHY IT WORKS

A reaction – oxidation – takes place between oxygen in the air and chemicals in the apple, and causes the surface to go brown. Acid in the lemon juice reacts with chemicals in the apple, slows down the oxidation and helps to keep the apple fresh.

Because oxygen is in the air and air is all around us, oxidation is a chemical reaction that is constantly taking place. Where it is damaging, we can take steps to stop it from happening.

45

Glossary

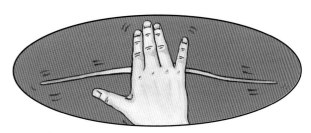

Atom
The smallest complete particle from which everything is made.

Chemical reaction
When two or more chemicals react to produce a chemical change.

Density
The weight, or heaviness, of an object per unit of volume. A litre of water weighs more than a litre of air, so it is more dense.

Electrolysis
A chemical change produced by passing an electric current through a substance. Electrolysis is used to coat cutlery with copper or silver.

Ion
A particle that is electrically charged. The particle can have a positive or a negative charge.

Microbe
A tiny living thing. Yeast is a microbe. Microbes are also known as microorganisms.

Molecule
A particle that contains two or more atoms joined together. Molecules of water each contain two atoms of hydrogen and one atom of oxygen.

Oxidation
A chemical reaction that needs oxygen to work. For example, iron is oxidised to a new chemical – iron oxide – when there is oxygen present. Iron oxide is also known as rust.

Phase change
When a substance undergoes a change from one phase to another. For example, when chocolate melts and changes from a solid to a liquid, or when water evaporates from a liquid to a gas.

Physical change

When chemicals interact with each other in a way that changes their physical structure. For example, when slime is made, the Borax makes the PVA glue tangle up and trap water in its tangles. The glue hasn't changed its chemical make up, but its physical structure has changed.

Polymer

A long chain of molecules that makes up a chemical. Plastic is made up of polymers.

Rubbing alcohol

A liquid that contains a chemical called isopropyl alcohol. Some nail varnish removers contain isopropyl alcohol and will also work in the experiments in this book. Don't touch or inhale either of these liquids as they can be harmful.

Silly Putty

A strange rubber-like substance that was invented by mistake in 1943 by James Wright. It is a polymer and is sold as a children's toy.

Solution

A fluid in which one substance has dissolved completely in another one.

Surface tension

The skin found on the surface of a liquid. Chemicals like washing up liquid break the surface tension.

Suspension

A substance whose particles are mixed with, but undissolved in, a fluid or solid. For example, custard is a suspension. The solid grains of custard hang in the water to make the suspension.

Index